Blue Banner Biography

Chris Daughtry

Kathleen Tracy

Mitchell Lane
PUBLISHERS

P.O. Box 196
Hockessin, Delaware 19707
Visit us on the web: www.mitchelllane.com
Comments? email us: mitchelllane@mitchelllane.com

Printing   1   2   3   4   5   6   7   8   9

Blue Banner Biographies

Akon	Alan Jackson	Alicia Keys
Allen Iverson	Ashanti	Ashlee Simpson
Ashton Kutcher	Avril Lavigne	Bernie Mac
Beyoncé	Bow Wow	Britney Spears
Carrie Underwood	Chris Brown	**Chris Daughtry**
Christina Aguilera	Christopher Paul Curtis	Ciara
Clay Aiken	Condoleezza Rice	Daniel Radcliffe
David Ortiz	Derek Jeter	Eminem
Eve	Fergie (Stacy Ferguson)	50 Cent
Gwen Stefani	Ice Cube	Jamie Foxx
Ja Rule	Jay-Z	Jennifer Lopez
Jessica Simpson	J. K. Rowling	Johnny Depp
JoJo	Justin Berfield	Justin Timberlake
Kate Hudson	Keith Urban	Kelly Clarkson
Kenny Chesney	Lance Armstrong	Lindsay Lohan
Mariah Carey	Mario	Mary J. Blige
Mary-Kate and Ashley Olsen	Michael Jackson	Miguel Tejada
Missy Elliott	Nancy Pelosi	Nelly
Orlando Bloom	P. Diddy	Paris Hilton
Peyton Manning	Queen Latifah	Ron Howard
Rudy Giuliani	Sally Field	Selena
Shakira	Shirley Temple	Tim McGraw
Usher	Zac Efron	

Library of Congress Cataloging-in-Publication Data
Tracy, Kathleen.
  Chris Daughtry / by Kathleen Tracy.
     p. cm. — (Blue banner biographies)
  Includes bibliographical references (p.   ), discography (p.   ), and index.
  ISBN 978-1-58415-629-1 (library bound)
  1. Daughtry, Chris, 1979– —Juvenile literature. 2. Rock musicians—United States—Biography—Juvenile literature. I. Title.
  ML3930.D325T73 2008
  782.42166092—dc22
  [B]

2007019792

ABOUT THE AUTHOR: Kathleen Tracy has been a journalist for over twenty years. Her writing has been featured in magazines including *The Toronto Star's Star Week, A&E's Biography magazine, KidScreen* and *Variety*. She is also the author of numerous biographies and other nonfiction books, including *Mariano Guadalupe Vallejo, William Hewlett: Pioneer of the Computer Age, The Watergate Scandal, The Life and Times of Cicero, Mariah Carey, Kelly Clarkson,* and *The Plymouth Colony: The Pilgrims Settle in New England* for Mitchell Lane Publishers. She divides her time between homes in Studio City and Palm Springs, California.

PHOTO CREDITS: Cover, p. 4—Ethan Miller/Getty Images; p. 7—*American Idol;* p. 8—Vince Bucci/Getty Images; p. 12—Daughtry; p. 15—Luis Martinez/AP Photo; p. 17—Jordan Strauss/WireImage; p. 20—Paul Hawthorne/Getty Images; p. 22—Soren McCarty/WireImage; p. 25—Tom Hauck/Getty Images; p. 27—Chris Gordon/Getty Images.

Blue Banner Biography

Chris Daughtry had reason to celebrate at the 2006 Billboard Music Awards. His first album, **Daughtry**, debuted at number one on Billboard's album charts and sold more than one million copies in a little over a month. Almost overnight Chris went from struggling artist to one of music's hottest talents. "I've accepted my new beginnings," he said.

The Shocker

*F*or once, even Simon Cowell was left speechless.

On May 10, 2006, Chris Daughtry stood beside Katharine McPhee on the *American Idol* stage. One of them would be going home. Most of the audience — and the judges — assumed it would be McPhee. When host Ryan Seacrest announced Daughtry had been voted off, it sparked a gasp heard 'round the country.

While emotional judge Paula Abdul cried on camera, Daughtry fans flocked to the Internet by the tens of thousands to express their disappointment, anger — and suspicions. Some questioned the validity of the vote tabulation. Others suggested that votes for Daughtry had intentionally been given to another contestant. But Chris had another explanation.

"Maybe people thought I was safe. . . . You know, I had a good night. . . . My voice was fine," he said. His performance of the week before had been a struggle vocally. "This week it was vocally one of the easiest weeks I've had. The keys of the songs were perfect for me. . . . My wife is the first one to criticize me and normally she agrees with Simon 100 percent, and last week she was like, 'You know that wasn't the right song for you to do.' I was disagreeing with her, like husbands always do. But this week she was like, 'I don't understand.'

"I think people may have gotten a little comfortable," he continued. "People thought, 'This guy is definitely going to win, I don't need to vote for him tonight.'"

During a press conference call the next day, Daughtry admitted that he was still trying to accept the elimination, which had caught him completely by surprise. "I was pretty shocked. I'm bummed. I'm disappointed—it's rough."

> *"I was pretty shocked. I'm bummed. I'm disappointed— it's rough."*

What made his abrupt departure that much more difficult is that Daughtry had emerged as the frontrunner to win. "I'm not trying to sound overconfident," he promised *Entertainment Weekly*. "But everyone had been telling me . . . even the judges said it was going to be a Chris-and-Taylor [Hicks] finale. You try not to buy into that, but when you hear it so much you think, 'Maybe they're right. Maybe I do have a good shot.'

"My hopes were up. I was starting to see there's an opportunity to win this thing. And then to have that happen was gut-wrenching."

In the aftermath, some viewers blamed the judges, but Cowell turned the table back on them, saying Daughtry's

*Many fans consider **American Idol**'s fifth season one of the series' best, with the most talented pool of contestants. In addition to Daughtry and eventual winner Taylor Hicks (third row, fourth from the right), Kellie Pickler (between Hicks and Daughtry) went on to begin a successful country career.*

fans may have taken too much for granted. "You would think it was us who voted him off," he told *Reality TV Magazine*. "We were . . . supporting him, and the public didn't put him through. The public, they control this show.

"If we had our way, we would bring him back, and then we would say to one of the finalists next week that it was a joke, you're not in the final. Good news and bad news, the bad news is you're not here, the good news is you've got a seat in the audience."

But the vote was final and there would be no reprieve. Chris tried to see his musical glass as half full. "You know,

Chris had to put his disappointment aside to perform on the **Idol** *season finale. Now, he says, "I look at those interviews and . . . I look like a miserable dude who just lost his life. I mean, that's what I was feeling at the time, I wasn't too happy about it."*

life goes on. I can't say I'm happy about it. It's definitely a very big disappointment for me but I'm trying to see the bigger picture and see that there's going to be bigger opportunities. It's one of those things that makes you stronger. You have to take it and run with it."

Daughtry told writer Jessica Shaw he was taking Cowell's words of encouragement to heart. "He said, 'You're obviously very talented. You need to keep going with that. You're going to be okay.' Randy [Jackson] said the same thing. . . . I'm grateful for what I was able to do, for the way the fans took to me and were so accepting of my style. I have to look at it like maybe it was the best thing for me. I have to realize God has a bigger plan."

Daughtry didn't have to wait long to get a glimpse of what that plan might be. On the TV show *Extra,* bass player Jeff Abercrombie and guitarist Carl Bell from the rock band Fuel publicly offered Chris a job as their lead singer. After Daughtry sang the Fuel song "Hemorrhage (In My Hands)" on *Idol* earlier in the competition, rumors had circulated that the band was interested in him. And in fact, he had secretly auditioned for them. Now they were ready to make it official.

"Chris, if you are watching, we've talked about this before," Abercrombie said. "And if you want to entertain it again we'll take it and go."

"He's perfect for Fuel," the band's manager Paul Geary told *People.* "He has the right voice, the right look."

Daughtry was faced with the most important professional decision of his career. "I'm just thinking everything through and making sure that I make the right decision for me and my family," he said.

Nobody, not even his wife, knew what Chris would decide. Whatever the decision, Chris Daughtry's life would never be the same.

> *"I'm just thinking everything through and making sure that I make the right decision for me and my family."*

Small-Town Boy

*C*hristopher Adam Daughtry was born December 26, 1979, in Roanoke Rapids, North Carolina. He and his brother Kenneth, who is three years older, grew up in nearby Lasker—a town so small there are only around 100 residents. In that rural area filled with rivers and forests, Chris told *USA Today* he remembers picking potatoes and corn "ever since we could walk." His parents, James (who goes by the nickname Pete) and Sandra, also raised chickens, ducks, goats, and hunting dogs on their land, which was situated next door to Chris's paternal grandparents, Calvin and Barbara Jean.

When he was thirteen, Chris got his first job, working with his dad at a local sawmill, admitting later, "I don't think it was legal." A year later, he took a safer job at McDonald's. But in 1994, his parents moved to the equally small Troy, Virginia, outside of Charlottesville. Located two hours southwest of Washington, D.C., Charlottesville holds an important place in American history. Named after King

George III's wife, Princess Sophia Charlotte, the city is best known as the location of Monticello, Thomas Jefferson's family plantation. Charlottesville is also home to the University of Virginia, founded by Jefferson.

Kenneth, who was eighteen and had a job, stayed behind in North Carolina while Chris moved with his parents to their new home. Chris enrolled at Fluvanna County High School in nearby Palmyra. It was there that he developed his interest in performing.

As he would later tell *Rolling Stone,* in high school, he "always wanted to be a comic artist. And I wanted to be the next Jean-Claude Van Damme, a martial-arts actor."

But he also liked being on stage and was active in his high school's drama department. He was cast as Smee in *Peter Pan* and appeared as the scarecrow in a production of *The Wiz.* His drama teacher, David Small, said that Chris took a particular interest in stage combat and even attended seminars on it. He was good enough that Small asked him to appear in a video he shot and still uses for teaching stage combat.

> *"[I] always wanted to be a comic artist. And I wanted to be the next Jean-Claude Van Damme, a martial-arts actor."*

The thing Small remembered most about his former student was that "Chris had a lot of stage presence. He was a director's actor. He always offered up a lot of things. Rather than us telling him what to do, he would throw stuff out, and from that he would mold it and work it. He knew how to work the audience."

The original band Daughtry, from left to right:
Josh Steely (guitar); Joey Barnes (drums);
Josh Paul (bass); Jeremy Brady (guitar); Chris
Daughtry (lead vocals). In 2007, Jeremy Brady left
the band and was replaced by Brian Craddock.

When he was sixteen, Daughtry's interests turned to music after he and his friend Robert got an assignment to write a song for their algebra class. Chris says it was the first time anyone told him he was a good singer.

"We had to write a song for class, so I forced myself to sing in front of him," he posted on a web site a few years later. "I always enjoyed singing but never had the confidence that Robert gave me that day. We wrote a couple songs and I was hooked. I knew at that time, that's what I wanted to do with my life. He taught me some guitar chords and I took off from there."

While in high school, Chris formed two bands, Benign and Cadence, and performed at Fluvanna's spring festival, Fluco Fest, to less than rave reviews.

"They were loud," teacher Jason Davis recalled to the *Fluvanna Review.*

Art teacher Diane Greenwood diplomatically called Chris "more artistic than musical."

Undaunted, Daughtry kept practicing. After graduating in 1998, he opted against college to pursue his music career. He supported himself with a series of retail jobs, and Cadence performed whenever they could. But in April 2000, Chris's life took an unexpected turn.

While visiting his brother, Kenneth, and his sister-in-law, Tracey, in 1999, Chris had met a divorced mother of two named Deanna Robertson at a party. Six months later, in April 2000, they married.

Even though he was only twenty, Chris said the idea of settling down with a wife and two young children—Hannah, then a year and a half old, and four-month-old Griffin—didn't scare him. "I felt like I didn't need to look anymore, that this was the person I was supposed to be with," he told *Life.com.* "If you know that, then you just go with it."

> "I felt like I didn't need to look anymore, that this was the person I was supposed to be with."

Chris disbanded Cadence and moved back to North Carolina, where Deanna owned a home in McLeansville. To support his new family, he got a job as a service worker at Crown Honda in nearby Greensboro. Although he never gave up his dream of being a performer, at times it would seem like an impossible quest.

New Band, Same Results

By all accounts Chris is an attentive, loving dad, although he admits that fatherhood was a far tougher challenge than trying to make it as a singer. But it was also more rewarding—Daughtry said one of his proudest moments was teaching Griffin to ride a bike. Meanwhile, he still hungered to perform.

While Chris was holding down a 9-to-5 job at the car dealership, rock and roll continued to be his passion. In 2004 he became lead singer and rhythm guitarist for a Birmingham, North Carolina–based rock band called Absent Element. Even though it took time away from the kids, Deanna was supportive.

"When we got married, I took on the two kids as my own. So, you know, she was . . . scared that I was sacrificing my dream by doing that," Chris explained on the band's web site. He said Deanna "was just really excited that I'm still gettin' to live it; that even though I took on the married

Less than two years after graduating from high school, Chris married Deanna Robertson and became a dad to her two young children. Chris credits his family with helping him get through stressful weeks on **American Idol.** *"It's always great to have that support. It was tough, but we made it through."*

life and the family early, that I'm still able to live my dream."

Being in the band helped Chris refocus his efforts. "Though I've always enjoyed singing, I was never pushed until I was in a rock band. Therefore it took years to develop the strength and range it takes to deliver Absent Element's screaming sound. My songwriting comes straight from the heart. I write about my relationship with God, my wife (who inspires most of my lyrics), and other life experiences. If it didn't happen to me, I can't effectively and honestly write about it."

> "Though I've always enjoyed singing, I was never pushed until I was in a rock band."

Chris says his musical influences are all over the Top 40 map. When he was fourteen he listened "to all the Nineties bands: Bush, Live, Alice in Chains' *Sap*, Soundgarden's *Superunknown*, STP [Stone Temple Pilots]. It just had this honesty to it that sucked me in," he told *Rolling Stone*.

As he got older, "I went through the whole Eighties thing with Guns n' Roses and Skid Row . . . and Rick Astley and Ace of Base. I also went through my rap phase with Public Enemy, N.W.A., and License to Ill . . . and you can't forget Vanilla Ice. Later, I became a big Elton John fan . . . and my wife turned me on to Led Zeppelin. Now I'll listen to the Killers or Fall Out Boy. But the stuff I go back to are those Nineties bands."

Absent Element played bars and clubs all around northeast North Carolina, sometimes playing to no more

Chris says it's important to vary his musical style. "I'm a singer. You can't sing the same song over and over. There's always a time and place to change things up, as long as you're being true to yourself."

than thirty people. After a while Chris began to wonder if the band would ever get the break they needed.

He told *Indyweek.com,* "I've been doing this since I was sixteen, and you get in a band, and you keep thinking, 'This is gonna be it. . . . But it's hard to convince yourself that you're bettering the family by going out every weekend and playing for twenty or thirty people." One time the band played a Saturday-morning gig in a nearly deserted parking lot.

Where they lived was a distinct disadvantage. "Where I live, nobody comes out to check out bands, especially people in the industry," he said in an AOL Sessions interview. "I had a family. I couldn't just get in a van, travel, get my face and name out there. We all had day jobs, we all had bills to pay. It was very difficult to get the exposure that I needed to make it."

"It was a real discouraging time," he admitted to *Entertainment Weekly*. "I always felt like, Next year we'll have a record deal. But years went by and nothing happened. It was horrible."

What made it especially frustrating was that Chris felt Absent Element was good enough to succeed. "I've been in several bands but have never experienced the chemistry that Absent Element share."

In 2005, Chris tried out for the CBS reality show *Rock Star: INXS.* The winner would become the new lead singer for the band and go on tour with them.

"When I heard they were coming to Charlotte, I sent them an audition tape," he recalled in *Rolling Stone.* "They emailed me immediately, and I got a private audition—no waiting in lines. Then I did 'Desire,' by U2. I don't think the band was digging my style too much."

Daughtry never made it past his audition, so he was less than enthusiastic when Deanna suggested he try out for *American Idol.* Chris admitted to writer Michael Endelman that his reaction was, "No way! It's too cheesy."

But a certain long-haired rocker would change his mind.

> *"I always felt like, Next year we'll have a record deal. But years went by and nothing happened. It was horrible."*

A Rocker
Emerges

*I*n McLeansville, Chris Daughtry was known as a good dad who often stopped by the kids' school to have lunch with them. "He's just normal," Deanna told *MSNBC*. "To a lot of people, he'd just seem boring." But, she added, "He's just a rocker at heart — always has been."

For years Deanna had been nudging him to audition for *American Idol.* "I always thought it was a little corny for what I was trying to do," he explained in Southern California's online paper, *Press-Enterprise.* "I didn't think it would cater to the rock community." But after seeing Bo Bice perform on the show, Chris had a change of heart and decided that maybe it was possible for a rock singer to do well on the show. "It was a risk, but I had to do it."

When the Season Five tryout cities were announced and included Memphis, Tennessee, Chris told Deanna he was going to audition. It wouldn't be easy. On the drive to Memphis, they learned the auditions had been canceled — so

Chris admits he's a bit of a perfectionist. "I put a lot of pressure on myself to make sure I put out what people want and expect out of me. I don't want to look back and not be proud of what I did."

he bought plane tickets for the next city on the list, Denver, Colorado.

"And when I got home I found out they'd added a new audition fifteen minutes from my house," Daughtry laughingly told the *Alameda Times-Star*. When he arrived in Denver for the audition, he was taken aback by the number of hopefuls.

"It was a little intimidating. There were 9,000 people outside. I thought, 'How am I gonna stand out?' "

Chris performed Joe Cocker's "The Letter" and

advanced — despite Simon Cowell's thumbs down. He felt Chris had been too robotic, but Randy Jackson and Paula Abdul pushed him through. Next stop: Hollywood.

Although he was pleased at making the cut, he later told Tom Lanham that he was suffering from some pre-trip homesickness. That was the inspiration for the song "Home."

"I came up with 'Home' about a month before I left to go to Hollywood. I was just sitting on the couch, thinking about what I was about to do, and I'd never been away from my family for that long, and the song just came out. I wrote it in five or ten minutes."

Once in Hollywood, it was clear Daughtry wasn't a typical *Idol* contestant. Week after week, regardless of the type of song he sang, he never hid his rock roots.

"I love ballads; just stuff that I can chill out with and really sing," he later explained on AOL Sessions. "But when I was on *Idol,* I wanted to take every opportunity to show that I was a rock singer and that if I was gonna make an album, this is the kind of music I'd put out. I wanted to make sure I got my voice heard and to make the biggest impact I could."

"I wanted to make sure I got my voice heard and to make the biggest impact I could."

Nor did any of the criticisms he received make him second-guess himself.

"You have to have a thick skin," he acknowledged in *USA Today.* "Nothing on the show hurt my confidence. Part of that is knowing who you are. If you don't know who you

Chris wrote "Home" a month before traveling to L.A. for **Idol.** *"I guess I started picturing what it was going to be like if things go really well. I wrote the song in ten minutes and I never changed anything from that time. I was really proud of it. It was just one of those songs that you're feeling it, and it came right out and you never really had to think about it."*

are, it's harder to be consistent, because you'll keep changing to please a certain judge. Then nobody knows who you are. They're trying to figure out which is the real you. I made sure that didn't happen. That's one reason I did so well. I didn't let them sway me or change me in any way. I think that's the key to anything in life: You have to know who you are."

One thing Chris wanted people to know was that he wasn't just a singer. "People get the impression that when you go on the show, you can sing, and that's about it. You're not really allowed to show whether or not you can play or whether or not you can write. You're just up there showing if you can sing that song good."

After his March 1, 2006, performance of Fuel's "Hemorrhage (In My Hands)" got rave reviews from all three judges, Daughtry suddenly became one of the favorites to win the competition. And then on May 10 came his stunning elimination. His friends and family in North Carolina were bitterly disappointed on his behalf, but it was Deanna who put it in perspective for him.

"I was really expecting her to be really out of control and I was going to have to be the one to console her," Chris admitted on *RealityTV.com.* "But . . . it was the other way around." After telling him how proud she was of him, Deanna told him that "things happen for a reason and we just have to hang on and see what that is and see that there's a bigger picture there."

It was that bigger picture that prevented Chris from jumping at the offer to be Fuel's new lead singer. During a welcome home party in North Carolina, Chris announced he was turning them down.

> *"Things happen for a reason and we just have to hang on and see what that is and see that there's a bigger picture there."*

"Deep down, I knew it wasn't for me," he told writer Edna Gundersen. "I wasn't comfortable being the guy who replaced the other guy or being limited to their success. I wanted to create my own. If I failed, I could blame myself."

He wouldn't fail.

Daughtry

*T*he shock of being eliminated had barely begun to wear off when Chris was told legendary record producer Clive Davis wanted to meet with him. The singer says he made one thing clear to Davis: "I told him I wanted to make sure that I was known as a band," Daughtry told the *New York Times*. "I didn't want to be a solo artist. That's never been what I was about. It was never an option."

Which is why, once he was able to look at his *Idol* experience objectively, Chris realized that not winning was the best thing that could have happened to his career.

"I don't feel like I would have been able to do what I wanted to do with my career," he explained to writer Sarah Linder. "I would have been a solo artist. It would have been an album that I probably would have regretted. . . . I think it would have stomped on my credibility a little bit."

Chris was finally getting the opportunity that had always eluded him: to truly make his own music for a national audience. "As a songwriter, I felt I had a lot to say," he said

Although Chris prefers to sing with his band, he was honored to perform "The Star-Spangled Banner" in January 2007 before the National Football Conference Championship Game between the Chicago Bears and New Orleans Saints. He says, "My favorite artists are bands, and I wanted that. I wanted that group of guys that are real tight together. It's not about one person—it's a group."

during an AOL Sessions interview. "This was my shot to go out and do my own thing."

Not only did fronting a band allow him to maintain his rock music integrity, Chris believes it also made him a better performer. "I'm a tough music fan myself," he says on his official web site. "I'm not swayed easily, but one of the things I've always loved about great bands is you feed off each other's confidence, build on each other's strengths, and create an opportunity for something magical to happen every time you go out there."

Chris announced his deal with 19 Entertainment in July and soon after handpicked a group of seasoned musicians that joined him to form Daughtry. Joey Barnes would be on drums and vocals, Josh Paul on bass, Josh Steely on lead guitar, and Jeremy Brady on guitar. (In January 2007, Brian Craddock would replace Jeremy.) They wrote material for their upcoming album while Chris was touring with the twelve *American Idol* finalists in the summer of 2006.

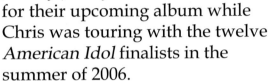

"Looking back now, sure, it was risky. But I never had the feeling that I was heading creatively somewhere where I shouldn't have been going."

"Looking back now, sure, it was risky. But I never had the feeling that I was heading creatively somewhere where I shouldn't have been going."

On November 21, the band's self-titled album, *Daughtry*, debuted at number one on the Billboard charts. In a little over five weeks, it had sold over a million copies, making it the fastest-selling rock debut album in Soundscan history. It would eventually be certified double platinum.

"The way it all has unfolded is everything an artist could ever ask for," Chris said in a post on the web site. "The guys have worked out beyond even what I had envisioned."

So have the fans. "It's such a blessing to receive all the great feedback and affection from the fans. The online intensity, the way they sing along at our shows, the radio and video support—I don't think the average person understands how crucial it is for a band to know you've got that net underneath you.

*Daughtry performs at SunFest 2007 in Florida. He calls his debut album, **Daughtry**, "the kind of album I've always wanted to make. It's got the sensitive, lighter stuff, but also the stuff that makes you want to run around in circles, pounding the walls in or something. I think it captures everything that I like about music."*

"To start out as a fan with a dream, and then to go from a struggling musician with the same hopes and aspirations as so many others and to be able to fulfill some of those dreams, well, I feel like we're all part of this incredible movement. I'm so aware of what it took to get here. I can't help but appreciate what an honor it is to keep it rolling."

> "I'm so aware of what it took to get here. I can't help but appreciate what an honor it is to keep it rolling."

Success has allowed Chris to buy a bigger, more private home for Deanna and their children. But it has also brought challenges, both professional and personal. Being on the road touring has tested the strength of his marriage. "I'm not there to help her with anything," he admitted in *Entertainment Weekly*. "I'm not there if she needs me."

Equally frustrating is being unable to shake the *Idol* connection. "I think that every artist wants to break away. You can't force it, though. You can't say, 'Don't call me Chris from *American Idol*.' That's going to have to happen on its own."

But Chris believes the sacrifices he and his family are making now will ensure his musical longevity. "I wanna look back twenty years from now and still be in the game in a big way," he told Sarah Linder. "I wanna be . . . a very important part of the music industry, whether it be playing or developing other bands. I would still honestly like to be performing every night and doing what I love to do."

So far, Chris Daughtry is on track to do just that.

CHRONOLOGY

1979   Christopher Adam Daughtry is born on December 26

1994   Moves with his parents to Troy, North Carolina

1996   Starts learning to play the guitar

1998   Graduates from Fluvanna County High School

1999   Meets his Deanna Robertson at a party

2000   Marries Deanna in November; moves to McLeansville, North Carolina, and gets a job with Crown Honda; performs at the Albemarle County Fair in August

2004   Becomes lead singer for Absent Element

2005   Tries out for *Rock Star: INXS*

2006   Auditions for *American Idol* in Denver, Colorado, and goes to Hollywood; is eliminated from *Idol* on May 10; announces record deal with 19 Entertainment on July 10; buys new house in Oak Ridge, North Carolina, for more privacy in August; first album, *Daughtry,* is released November 21; *Daughtry* is certified double platinum

2007   Performs "Star-Spangled Banner" at NFC Championship Game in January; begins sold-out concert tour in March

Album

2006   *Daughtry*

Singles

2007   "It's Not Over"

2006   "Home"

Books

While no other books on Chris Daughtry are available, you might enjoy these other Blue Banner Biographies from Mitchell Lane Publishers:

Granados, Christine. *Christina Aguilera.* Hockessin, Delaware: Mitchell Lane Publishers, Inc., 2005.

Torres, John A. *Clay Aiken.* Hockessin, Delaware: Mitchell Lane Publishers, Inc., 2005.

Tracy, Kathleen. *Avril Lavigne.* Hockessin, Delaware: Mitchell Lane Publishers, Inc., 2005.

Tracy, Kathleen. *Carrie Underwood.* Hockessin, Delaware: Mitchell Lane Publishers, Inc., 2006.

Tracy, Kathleen. *Gwen Stefani.* Hockessin, Delaware: Mitchell Lane Publishers, Inc., 2007.

Tracy, Kathleen. *Kelly Clarkson.* Hockessin, Delaware: Mitchell Lane Publishers, Inc., 2007.

Works Consulted

Endelman, Michael. "The Anti-Idol." *Entertainment Weekly.*
http://www.ew.com/ew/article/0,,20011924,00.html

Guiden, Mary. "Living the Life of an Idol, Even Without the Title."
Seattle Times, February 2, 2007, p. H4.

Gunderson, Edna. "It's Just Beginning for Chris Daughtry." *USA
Today.* March 20, 2007. http://www.usatoday.com/life/
music/news/2007-03-20-chris-daughtry-main_N.htm

Lanham, Tom. "Daughtry Trades Reality TV for Concert Stage."
Alameda Times-Star. February 2, 2007.

Linder, Sarah. Chris Daughtry interview, January 31, 2007,
http://www.austin360.com/blogs/content/shared-gen/
blogs/austin/americanidol/entries/2007/01/31/

Oldenburg, Ann. "Daughtry: I Was Pretty Shocked." *USA Today*
May 11, 2006. http://www.usatoday.com/life/television/
news/2006-05-11-daughtry-interview_x.htm

Sculley, Alan. "Idol Kicked Off Career." *The Press-Enterprise.*
January 26, 2007, p. AA03.

Scaggs, Austin. "Q&A: Chris Daughtry." *Rolling Stone.* http://
www.rollingstone.com/artists/chrisdaughtry/articles/
story/13903019/qa_and_exclusive_audio_chris_daughtry

Shaw, Jessica. "The Biggest Idol Ever." *Entertainment Weekly.*
April 21, 2006.

Shaw, Jessica. "A Little More Conversation." *Entertainment Weekly.*
http://www.ew.com/ew/article/0,,1193305,00.html

Sisaro, Ben. "Creating a New Reality, And a String of Hit Songs."
New York Times, March 22, 2007, p. 3.

On the Internet

Daughtry, Official Site
http://www.daughtryofficial.com

Chris Daughtry Web
http://www.chrisdaughtryweb.com/about.html

INDEX